LIFE'S LITTLE RELAXATION BOOK

by Steven Michael Selzer

LIFE'S LITTLE RELAXATION BOOK

Crown Trade Paperback
New York

Copyright © 1994, 1995 by Steven Michael Selzer

All rights reserved. No part of this book may be reproduced or transmitted in any form or by any means, electronic or mechanical, including photocopying, recording, or by any information storage and retrieval system, without permission in writing from the publisher.

Published by Crown Trade Paperbacks, 201 East 50th Street, New York, New York 10022. Member of the Crown Publishing Group.

Portions of this book were previously published by S.P.I. Books, a division of Shapolsky Publishers, Inc., in 1994.

Random House, Inc. New York, Toronto, London, Sydney, Auckland

CROWN TRADE PAPERBACKS and colophon are trademarks of Crown Publishers, Inc.

Manufactured in the United States of America

Design and illustrations by Evelyn Kim

Library of Congress Cataloging-in-Publication Data
Selzer, Steven Michael.
Life's little relaxation book / Steven Michael Selzer.—1st ed.
Originally published: New York: S.P.I. Books, c1994
1. Stress (Psychology) 2. Stress management. I. Title.
BF575.S75S45   1995
155.9'042—dc20   95-559
CIP

ISBN 0-517-88483-6

10 9 8 7 6 5 4 3

This book is dedicated to the memory of Nathan J. Selzer.

ACKNOWLEDGMENTS

The relaxed and supportive attitudes of my wife, Adrianne, and my sons,
Ethan and Elliott, are appreciated. I wish to thank Mr. Alan Sultan,
the catalyst for the second printing of this book.

Additionally, Ms. Deborah Grosvenor, my agent, has been very helpful
in her guidance and direction. Ms. Valerie Kuscenko, my editor, has added focus
and universality to this book for which I am grateful. Her efforts go beyond the call
of duty. The enthusiasm of Ms. Adrienne Ingram is appreciated as well. I wish to
thank Wendy Hubbert for her energetic coordinating efforts to bring forth this
book in a sensible, effective way.

PREFACE

It is essential to reduce stress. We all build up stress. There are only three recovery systems: sleeping well, eating properly, and relaxation.

The purpose of *Life's Little Relaxation Book* is to help reduce stress with the suggestion of simple, inexpensive ways to relax. These methods do not involve special training. They may be employed on a daily basis. They work.

My hope is that you will use these ideas to relax. In so doing, you will recover from the stress we all experience. Enjoy this book, and relax!

Steven Michael Selzer
Rockville, Maryland 1995

LIFE'S LITTLE RELAXATION BOOK

Keep a *positive attitude*—
anticipate the good things that are just around the corner.

Go to a

"*learn-to-massage*"

class with your partner.

12   Sit in a chair OVERLOOKING any place visited by boats.

13

Visit a *playground*
and ride on the *swings*.

On a lazy Sunday,
wear your *pajamas* all day.

It is not only kind
but relaxing to *help others*.

Dig your feet deep
in the *wet sand* at the beach.

Take *long walks* in natural settings with someone whose company you enjoy. 15

Learn and practice a few *magic tricks*.

Get to work a *half hour* earlier than necessary
to collect your thoughts before the day gets crazy.

Enjoy the feeling of a *manicure* or *pedicure*.

Listen to *soft music.*

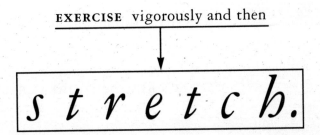

EXERCISE vigorously and then

stretch.

Do not discuss **POLITICS** with friends.

Savor soft, **FROZEN CUSTARD**—it is back.

WINDOW-SHOP—fun at no expense.

Stay at a **BED-AND-BREAKFAST** inn.

Keep things **UNCLUTTERED**.

*Keep the **television off** as much as possible,*
especially during dinnertime
with your family.

Squeeze and *knead* some Nordic Track *exercise* putty.

Visit your local library and
check out a *travel book* about a tropical location.

Construct or *assemble* something you would normally buy ready-made.

Stock *books on tape* in your car
to alleviate the stress of being confined
for a long period of time.

Take *family vacations,*
however brief.
Occasionally,
make it just
the *two of you.*

Engage in a sport or activity that allows you
TO RELEASE YOUR AGGRESSIONS.

| TRY RACQUETBALL |

you can hit a small ball as hard as you like.

Stay away from————————

Eat fondue
with a friend,
savor each bite.

overly competitive people.

25

DO NOT WORRY
about changing things that are beyond your control.

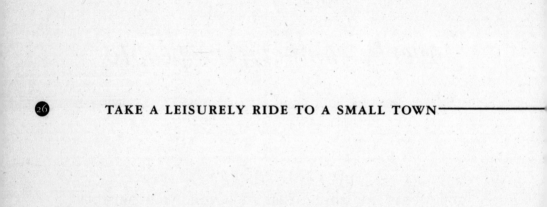

26   **TAKE A LEISURELY RIDE TO A SMALL TOWN** ─────

soak in the slow pace and appreciate the friendliness of the locals.

After a particularly stressful day,

EAT SOME PASTA FOR DINNER—

it is easy on the digestive system.

Equip yourself with a **GOOD ATLAS**.

Volunteer for a community-related committee or project—it will be enriching.

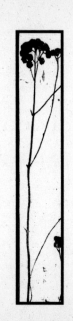

| CHERISH | the quiet of an early morning before the sun rises. **31**

Sit by a **LAKE**, **RIVER**, or **GURGLING STREAM**.

Stroll through a **PARK** that you had **FORGOTTEN**.

Have fun with your face
—change your glasses, grow a mustache or beard, change your makeup.

Go to the mountains, lake, or ocean
for a weekend anytime of the year
—it will seem like a **week-long vacation**.

When playing sports,
simply try to do your best
—**do not worry** about winning.

Hear people out————

34

Enjoy **compliments** you receive,
as well as those you give to others.

BOWLING CAN BE FUN NOW AND THEN.

DO NOT INTERRUPT.

Go to see
LIFE-AFFIRMING
movies.

35

Rent classic videos that hark back to **SIMPLER TIMES.**

Work out before going to the office

TO ENERGIZE

for the day.

Prioritize activities, and leave plenty of time for fun.

Arrive early for all meetings
and appointments.

Recognize that *good manners* and *grace*
are always in style.

When attending seminars,
sit up front.
KNOWLEDGE is power.

Extend *courtesies* on the road— it is so much more pleasant.

42   Solve problems by focusing on the *solution*,

not dwelling on the *problem*. [43]

READ

a good mystery
by the fireplace.

HIKE the nearest mountain.

Value *continuity*.

Rent a *canoe*.

Eat **NATURAL FOODS**.

Attend a minor league baseball game—inexpensive and fun.

Stargaze **on a clear evening.**

HONOR

→ friendship.

If your lawn is small enough,
push your *hand mower*————

there's no need to be

MOTORIZED.

Make your life as *festive* as possible.

52 GO TO THE *ZOO*.

Reread your *favorite book*.

Appreciate the

INTERDEPENDENCE

we experience in this world.

54 *Be* **upbeat** *with everyone—
you're always listening to yourself.*

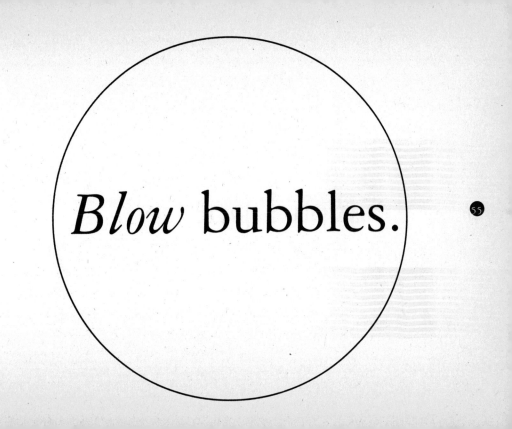

Blow bubbles.

55

Read poetry

seriously.

Start a weekly men's or women's group where you can *let down your guard* and *talk about your feelings*.

Rent a hotel room with a *waterbed* for the weekend.

Use your *fireplace*—keep *marshmallows* handy to roast.

Enhance your sense of self-worth—

by spending time with people who care about you.

62 Be comfortable with *silence*.

Take a long ⟶

bike ride on a path.

Read

Henry David Thoreau

under a tree.

64

Take a nap———

Watch old episodes of *I Love Lucy* and *Leave It to Beaver*.

Visit an *aquarium.*

→ in the afternoon.

Drink Celestial Seasonings *caffeine-free herb tea.*

Read to children

watch the expressions
on their faces.

Try your hand at *painting*, *sculpting*, or *drawing*.

Experience *sailing*.

Use music to *relax*.

Try *bird-watching*.

Sip *hot cider* on a cold day.

69

DO NOT ANGER EASILY

$\longrightarrow$ **BE FORGIVING.**

Gardening truly allows you to COMMUNE

Enjoy the sun in moderation.

Wear **COMFORTABLE**, loose cotton clothing.

⟶ with nature.

Visit with relatives or friends
who have *newborns*.

73

Sing along with
YOUR FAVORITE SONGS
on the radio.
Indulge in an occasional
ICE CREAM SUNDAE
or BANANA SPLIT.

Purchase a **MINI-POOL TABLE**, and play some pool.

Play *miniature golf* for fun.

76

Sleep with a comforter.

Till the soil,
then grow **VEGETABLES** in **YOUR GARDEN**.

it will make you more giving.

Limit your intake of *caffeine*.

Sip *tomato soup* on a *cold winter night*.

Read the *Sunday newspaper*
for at least half the morning.

Make nice to *your pet*.

Savor *ice pops* in the summer.

Attend *garage sales* early or late in the day.

Go to

⟶ the *beach*,

especially in the fall or winter.

Play *chess*.

Wear *old, soft jeans*.

Enjoy fiber-rich popcorn when **snacking**.

If we can recycle materials, we can **renew** ourselves.

Do not watch too much news on television ⎯⎯⎯

Barbecue year-round.

Give yourself positive feedback
and don't forget to smile.

→ you can **be selective** when reading the newspaper. 83

84 *Sing* oldies in the *shower*.

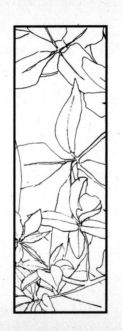

Play ball games

with your **kids**

when they are young.

Play catch with them

when they are a bit older.

Watch them **play**

after that.

Watch a *spider* spinning its *web*.

Pick *apples* in autumn.

Swim laps, but **do not count** how many you have done.

If you are the parent of a teenager,
remember that he or she is on

a temporary sojourn

→ only take a stand on the truly important issues.

Go **ice-skating** on a frozen pond.

Hit **golf balls** for fun—when playing do
not take the game too seriously.

Help a **shelter** in some way—contribute
food, clothing, or your time.

Take a **pleasurable thought** over
to your rocking chair.

Associate with **POSITIVE, UPBEAT PEOPLE**.

Appreciate *modern technology.*

| BE CONTENT | with
what you have.

Enjoy your *family* and *friends*—call them, get together.

Appreciate LIFE itself.

Eat slowly and ENJOY each morsel.

Yoga—Yogurt—Yo-yo.

ACCEPT that everyone has peculiarities.

Through examples
set by certain people
and demonstrated
in classic films,
teach manners
and graciousness
to your children
in a subtle way.

Stay in touch
with older friends and relations.

Fly a kite
on a windy afternoon in a treeless area.

Observe ***religious holidays*** with your family.

Rent a convertible—
drive to the country and feel the surroundings.

96 BE PATIENT WITH OTHERS AND YOURSELF.

DO NOt go to the horse races.

WHEN WATCHING YOUR CHILDREN PLAY SPORTS ——————

Soak in a **hot tub.**

be happy that they are healthy enough to be out there participating. **99**

Feel yourself *smile*— *see* how it affects others.

Take *photos* and *videos* of your family
regularly in an unobtrusive way.

Take a *lunch break* outside of your office
for at least *thirty minutes*.

When choosing *a pet*, look for one with
a calm and affectionate disposition.

FIX HOT CHOCOLATE.

Be other-directed———————

Set up a **RETIREMENT PLAN** and contribute to it as best you can.

Be **NEIGHBORLY**.

→ EMPATHIZE, DO NOT CRITICIZE.

After you have DONE ALL YOU CAN DO to improve a situation, forget about it.

Keep plants IF YOU ENJOY tending to their needs.

Enjoy a LITTLE WINE with dinner on occasion.

104   Be a person who gives and engenders **loyalty**.

Do not go to THE SUPERMARKET on Saturday afternoon.

106 If you are uncomfortable with a situation,

say **NO**.

DO NOT DWELL
in the past—
LIVE
for the present—
PLAN
for the future.

Go fishing with
low **expectations.**

Wear **flannel shirts**
in cold weather.

Rent a **classic jukebox** for a party to encourage dancing.

Keep things in perspective—**good health** and **peace of mind** are what **truly count**.

Have **hot pizza** delivered to be eaten slowly with family or friends at home.

Exercise vigorously

Try Para-Sailing—*it is otherworldly.*

at least *three times a week*.

Take long, hot *showers*—
let the stream of water massage
your neck and back muscles.

Smiling & laughter ease anxiety.

Occasionally relive the past and reminisce with *photos*.

Stop and take

A RENEWING DEEP BREATH

several times a day.

A good attitude is

contagious.

Add **CANDLELIGHT** to a romantic dinner.

Get in **BED** early on a winter's night.

Sip a long, **COOL LEMONADE** on a hot summer's day.

Spend an evening at a **COMEDY CLUB**.

Visit **WARMER CLIMATES** in the winter if possible.

Envelop your feet in soft, warm sweat socks.

Switch to *feather pillows*.

Read Robert Frost.

Close your eyes and think of a **serene place**.
Visit that place in your mind's eye.

Tickle your *sweetheart*.

Take a *bubble bath*.

Read—it is the fountain of wisdom.

Bake bread.

Feed the wild birds.

Instead of watching television,
listen to your **FAVORITE MUSIC**
with your eyes closed.

Try pitching **horseshoes**.

Uplift others with your **high spirits**.

Delight yourself occasionally with a **gift**.

Sing in a chorus or choir.

Seek occasional solitude to
spend time thinking

CONTRIBUTE regularly to your favorite charity.

CHALLENGE yourself with a good crossword puzzle.

BROADEN your musical tastes.

VISIT an art gallery.

⟶ | thoughts are a source of personal power. |

Indulge in
*some **chocolate mousse***
for dessert.

Own and browse *a good dictionary*.

Let it go

↓

| BE TOLERANT. |

Go *dancing* occasionally, even if you do not consider yourself to be a good dancer—it is an ancient way of *expressing joy* through movement.

After a long day,
use an *eye mask* that can be heated or chilled.

Go shopping at a *farmer's market*.

Learn and *keep current* in your field.

Go to the pond and *feed the ducks*,
but beware of the aggressive geese.

Peel some *string cheese* for a snack.

Make friends with a *computer*.

Go *horseback riding*.

Jog outside or on a treadmill indoors.

128 Attend *patriotic parades* with a flag in hand.

Crunch *caramel apples* at Halloween.

Relax in a *sauna*.

Find intriguing information in a fine encyclopedia.

Buy a **BACK AND NECK MASSAGER**
and put it to good use.

Add a **PORCH, DECK,** or **SUNROOF**
to **YOUR HOUSE**.

FROZEN FRUIT DRINKS
cool you off in the summer.

Go **ROLLER-SKATING** or **ROLLER-BLADING**
in a rink or in the park.

Play games with friends
or the kids—it's the *secret of perpetual youth*.

A crunchy cereal at breakfast helps you
slow down while eating.

Cut up a juicy, sweet watermelon in the summer.
Smell the sweetness in the air.

Listen to classical music in the car.

TAKE

→ a bubble gum break every once in a while.

Athletic shoes *with bounce* will
put spring in your step.

Enjoy a good *yawn* accompanied
by a good *stretch*.

Join a **tennis doubles team** with a friend or with a spouse.

Learn a few simple **sing-along tunes** on the piano.

Add oil and vinegar to your salad for **some zing**.

Drink some **old-fashioned draft root beer**.

Build SAND CASTLES.

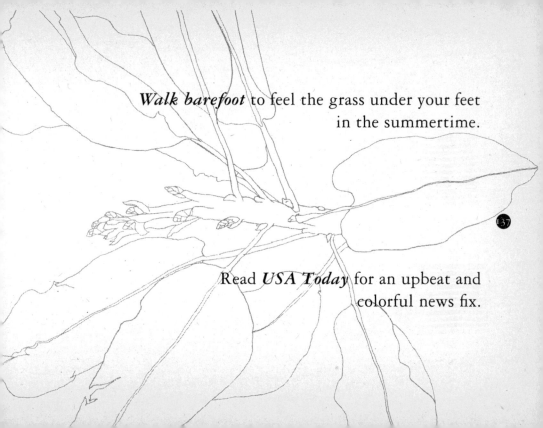

Walk barefoot to feel the grass under your feet
in the summertime.

Read *USA Today* for an upbeat and
colorful news fix.

There's a *moon* out tonight—

share *it* with someone.

Start a **collection** of anything you enjoy
→ *organize it, add to it.*

Make some *mashed potatoes* from *scratch*.

Rake the *leaves* instead of using a noisy blower.

Celebrate *birthdays* with *helium balloons*.

Swing in a *hammock*.

Eat *bagels* and *cream cheese*.

Treat yourself to a *facial*.

People-watch.

Give one dessert a year to pie *à la mode*.

Appreciate the vibrant colors of *changing leaves* in autumn.

Gaze at *tropical fish*.

Give a friend a *foot massage*.

Go *sledding* in winter.

Listen instead of just hearing.

WALK ON TRAILS IN THE WOODS.

Picnic.

Visit a *museum.*

Browse through a bookstore
or the public library ⌐
            └──▶ *really take your time.*

Don't shave on the weekend —————

Buy yourself a float or raft

for the ocean or lake

↓

you will enjoy the buoyancy.

TAKE A *nap* ON A RAINY DAY.

→ *give your skin a break.*

Hold *hands*.

Water your lawn or garden on an early *summer's morning*.

146   Send *roses* to the one you *love* for no special reason.

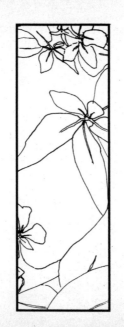

Visit *New York City* near the holiday season for a festive time.

Use an *organizing system*.

Experience a *scalp massage*.

Treat yourself to a pair of *flannel sheets*.

Give or get a *back rub*.

Put on your boots and take a walk in the first *heavy snow*.

Drink spring water——

IT'S STILL NATURE'S BEST BEVERAGE.

Host a *small dinner party* for your favorite couple.

Look through **OLD FAMILY PICTURE** albums.

Enjoy some **PRETZELS** for a low-fat snack.

Use **SKIN MOISTURIZER**.

Kissing your *loved ones*
can be fun.

Take the bicycles on a rack to a *scenic bike path*.

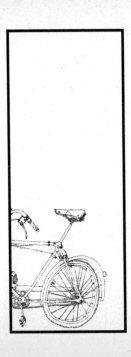

153

*Listen to the **rain pattering** on the roof.*

Savor
warm, soft

CHOCOLATE CHIP COOKIES

every now
and then.

<u>SEND GREETING CARDS OFTEN</u>

they help you keep in touch.

Cuddle in the winter.

Be dedicated to your job—*it's a matter of pride.*

Go to ⟶

a festive local street fair.

Basmati rice is very nice—
enjoy its wonderful aroma as it's cooking.

GIVE SMALL PRESENTS

frequently.

Watch your

favorite sporting events

to see some

exciting teamwork.

Try *fly-fishing*.

Visit *historic places*.

Keep a *tissue box* in every room and in the car.

Listen to a "*surf*" white-sound machine.

Smell the newly *mowed lawn*.

Try sleeping in a **NIGHTSHIRT**.

If you have the time,
organize your clothes
for the next morning.

Play *together*.

162 Write letters to relatives and friends————

——————▶ you will enjoy receiving them, too.

Massage your forehead.

Draw up a **FAMILY TREE**.

Books are the **PRESENTS** people keep opening.

Take the **PHONE** off the hook when possible.

Play **POOL** without placing bets.

Always talk out

↓

EMOTIONAL ISSUES.

When you're *feeling down*————

go somewhere and have a *good cry* to relieve the tension.

STOP rushing around——

Take time alone.

→ *some things can be*
put off until tomorrow.

Take a ferry ride.

NEVER

take yourself too seriously.

Wear a *cashmere scarf* to keep you warm.

Write a *list* before going to the supermarket.

Switch from stiff shoes to *soft moccasins*.

Go easy on the *cologne* or *perfume*.

Drive a *different route* to work.

Experience pure fun

↓

take off your shoes
and
run through a puddle.

SIP

174   a steaming mug of *Postum*———

a wholesome,

ALL-NATURAL BEVERAGE.

Visit the *planetarium*.

Do not sweat the *small stuff*.

Balance *work* and *family life*.

Only make *promises* you can keep.

Cherish *your family*, the one constant.